On Your Toes

A Ballet A B C

BY RACHEL ISADORA

GREENWILLOW BOOKS

An Imprint of HarperCollinsPublishers

A
Arabesque

B Backstage

C Costume

D

Développé

E
En pointe

F

Firebird

G

Grand jeté

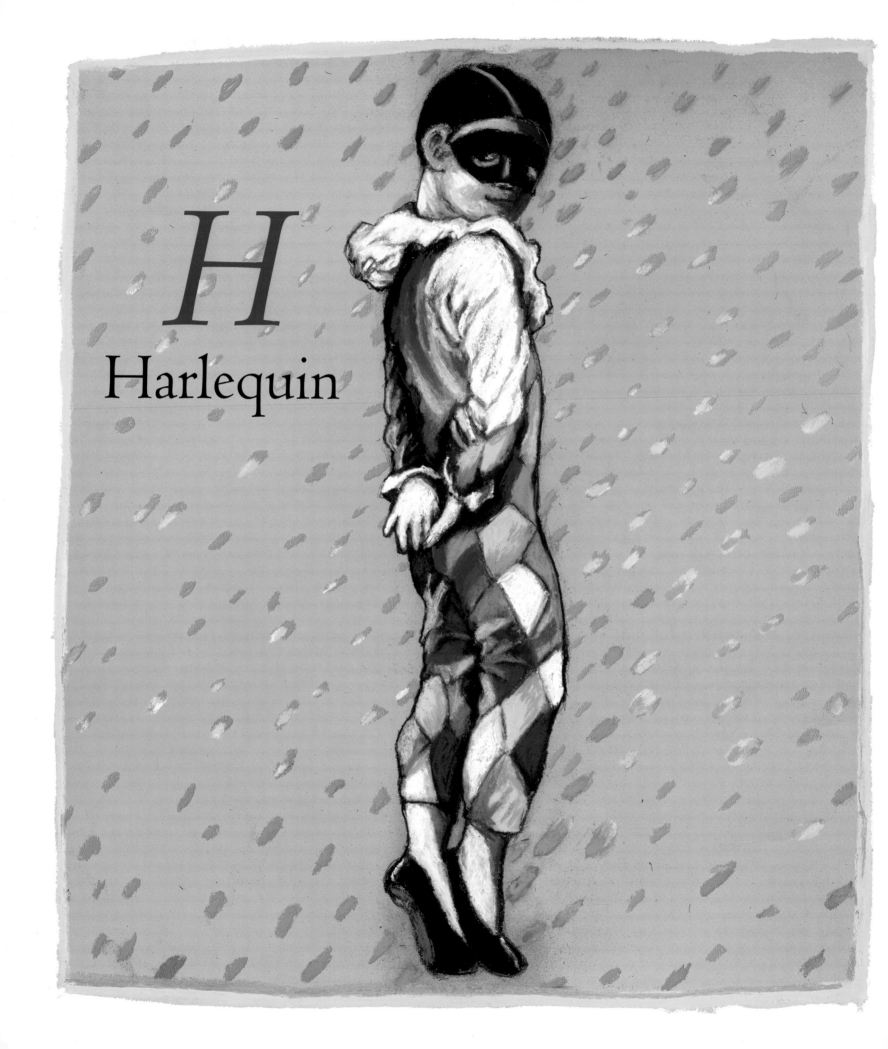

H

Harlequin

I
Instructor

J
Jump

K

Kiss

L
Lights

M

Makeup

N

Nutcracker

O

Odette

P

Pas de chat

Q
Queen

R

Révérence

S

Sleep

T

Tutu

U
Upside down

V
Variation

W

Warm-ups

X

X marks
the spot

Y

Yarn

Z
Zipper

Glossary

Arabesque (air-ah-BESK)—A pose in which the dancer stands on one leg and extends the other behind her, with a straight knee and pointed foot. This dancer is trying to keep her back straight, leg high, and balance steady, all at the same time.

Backstage—The place the audience doesn't see, where dancers and technicians prepare for the performance. Behind the scene, stagehands ready the stage, costumes hang on racks, and dancers warm up and wait for their cues to go onstage.

Costume—The clothes a dancer wears for a ballet. Ballet costumes are made from materials such as silk, satin, nylon, spandex, wool, and even plastic. Here, the dancer is a bug in the ballet *A Midsummer Night's Dream*. Her costume is flexible and lightweight so she can move easily.

Développé (dayv-lah-PAY)—A French word meaning "developing movement." Most ballet steps have French names because the first school for ballet opened in Paris in 1661. In this step, the dancer draws one foot up, touching her standing leg, then extends it. The dancer here is trying not to wobble and to keep her hips even.

En pointe (ahn PWANT)—A French term that means "on point." Ballet dancers wear special shoes that help them go up on their toes. Pointe, or toe, shoes have satin on the outside and layers of strong glue and fabric in the arch and on the toe. Most dancers put lambswool, tape, or pads over their toes for more cushioning. Being on point can be painful, and a dancer often develops corns, blisters, and bunions.

Firebird—A ballet that takes place in Russia. It was first performed in 1910 with music by Igor Stravinsky and choreography by Michel Fokine. The Firebird, a magical creature, presents Prince Ivan with a feather that saves the princess from an evil magician and his monsters.

Grand jeté (grahn zhuh-TAY)—A big jump from one foot to the other with the legs outstretched. It is very exciting to see dancers do this step because they look as if they are flying.

Harlequin—A comic, mischievous character who appears in many ballets. A harlequin often dances on demi-pointe, or on the balls of his feet, and does many jumps and turns.

Instructor—The ballet teacher who helps a student become a ballet dancer. It takes many years of studying to learn how to dance well. Most instructors were once dancers who performed with ballet companies.

Jump—A spring into the air from one or two legs. In ballet, there are many jump steps. In this picture, the dancers are doing the step called "changement de pieds" (shahnj-MAHN duh pee-AY), a French term that means "change of feet." They are trying to jump as high as they can while keeping their legs straight and toes pointed.

Kiss—In some ballets, the characters fall in love and kiss. In this picture Titania, Queen of the Fairies, kisses the donkey in the ballet *A Midsummer Night's Dream* and falls in love with him.

Lights—Powerful, bright, colored lights are used to illuminate the stage. These are called stagelights and are positioned backstage, above the stage, and around the theater. A spotlight focuses on one dancer or couple.

Makeup—A dancer uses special makeup for performing. Colors are brighter, eyelashes longer, and rouge darker so that the audience can see the dancer's features from far away. It takes a long time to learn how to put on stage makeup and what works best under the very bright lights.

The Nutcracker—A popular ballet first performed in 1892, with music by Peter Ilyitch Tchaikovsky and choreography by Lev Ivanov. Here, Marie and the prince are leaving the Land of Snow.

Odette—A princess under the evil spell of the magician Von Rothbart. He transforms her into a swan in the famous ballet *Swan Lake*. This ballet first opened in 1895, and it has music by Peter Ilyitch Tchaikovsky and choreography by Marisu Petipa and Lev Ivanov. The role of Odette remains one of the most cherished roles for a dancer to perform today.

Pas de chat (pah duh SHAH)—A French phrase meaning "step of the cat." This step is a jump in the air with both legs bent at the knee or with one leg extended. The dancer tries to land from the jump as quietly as possible, just like a cat.

Queen—A role in many classical ballets. The dancer in this role must stand straight and tall and look regal. Often, a dancer must act as well as dance.

Révérence (rev-air-AHNS)—A bow or curtsy usually done at the end of a class to thank the instructor. Here, the dancers are thanking each other after dancing together. This tradition dates back to the origins of ballet, when dancers performed in the courts of kings and queens.

Sleep—After hours of classes, rehearsals, and performances, sleep is very welcome. Dancers must eat well and get plenty of sleep in order to dance their best. The dancers try to take naps whenever they can, sometimes even backstage or in their dressing rooms.

Tutu—A ballet skirt, either short and fluffy or stretching to the calf or ankle, made of several layers of tulle or other fabric. Some tutus have jewels, beads, flowers, or ribbons sewn onto them. Originally, the tutu was the underskirt, and a skirt made of heavy fabric, such as velvet, was worn over it.

Upside down—A position of the body, demonstrated here in a backbend. Dancers do many stretches, such as backbends, which help them to be very flexible.

Variation—A solo dance in a ballet. It is exciting to dance onstage alone, but it takes many years of training and performing before a dancer is chosen to do this. Most dancers perform with other dancers in the main group of the ballet company, called the "corps de ballet" (kore duh BA-lay). This picture shows Prince Florimund in a variation from the ballet *Sleeping Beauty*.

Warm-ups—A series of exercises that all ballet dancers do to loosen their muscles. Without warm-ups, dancers could hurt themselves and not be able to perform. Stretches and splits are two of the ways a dancer limbers up.

X marks the spot—The mark that shows the place where a dancer must position herself or himself while onstage. The mark can be drawn on the stage or marked by tape. The stage is very dark during this scene in *The Nutcracker*, so the X shows the dancer where the center of the stage is.

Yarn—Leg warmers, used to keep the dancer's legs warm and supple, are made of knitted yarn. Some dancers knit their own leg warmers, and others buy them from stores that sell ballet supplies.

Zipper—A fastener that is sewn into a costume to close it. Hooks and eyes, Velcro, and buttons are used as well. Dancers must be able to get in and out of their costumes quickly because sometimes they will make six costume changes during a single performance.

For Gillian and Rita

On Your Toes: A Ballet ABC

Copyright © 2003 by Rachel Isadora Turner

All rights reserved.

Manufactured in China.

www.harperchildrens.com

Colored pastels were used to prepare the full-color art.

The text type is 50-point Centaur.

Library of Congress Cataloging-in-Publication Data

Isadora, Rachel.

On your toes : a ballet ABC / by Rachel Isadora.

p.   cm.

"Greenwillow Books."

Summary: Each letter of the alphabet is represented

by an illustration of a ballet-related word.

ISBN 0-06-050238-X (trade)

ISBN 0-06-050241-X (lib. bdg.)

1. Ballet—Juvenile literature. 2. Ballet dancing—Juvenile literature.

3. Alphabet books. [1. Ballet. 2. Alphabet.] I. Title.

GV1787.5.I74 2003 792.8—dc21 2002023549

4 6 8 10 9 7 5

First Edition

 GREENWILLOW BOOKS